India's Silent Revolution: Manmohan Singh's journey

S.RAI

Published by S.RAI, 2024.

INDIA'S SILENT REVOLUTION: MANMOHAN SINGH'S JOURNEY

First edition. December 28, 2024.

Copyright © 2024 S.RAI.

ISBN: 979-8230934714

Written by S.RAI.

Table of Contents

Dedication

To **Dr. Manmohan Singh**,

A leader of quiet strength, a visionary economist, and a statesman whose contributions have shaped modern India in ways that history will continue to recognize and appreciate. This book, *India Silent Revolution*, is dedicated to you—not just as an acknowledgment of your role in India's transformation, but as a tribute to the power of silent yet profound leadership.

At a time when the world often associates leadership with grand speeches and assertive rhetoric, your journey stands as a testament to the idea that real change can be brought about without noise, without unnecessary confrontation, and without the need for personal glorification. Your work has demonstrated that revolutions do not always have to be loud to be effective; sometimes, they unfold quietly, through policies, reforms, and the determination to push forward despite opposition.

A Visionary of Economic Reform

When you took charge as India's Finance Minister in 1991, the country was on the brink of an economic crisis. Foreign reserves were depleting at an alarming rate, inflation was skyrocketing, and the very foundation of India's economic policies needed restructuring. It was in this moment of crisis that you, along with Prime Minister P.V. Narasimha Rao, initiated a series of economic reforms that changed the course of India's history.

The liberalization, privatization, and globalization (LPG) policies introduced under your leadership dismantled decades of economic stagnation. With the removal of the License Raj, India welcomed private enterprise, opened up to foreign investments, and set itself on a path of unprecedented economic growth. These reforms were not just about numbers and policies; they fundamentally changed the lives of millions, offering new opportunities, new aspirations, and a newfound confidence in India's economic potential.

What makes your contribution even more remarkable is that these reforms were not driven by populism or political gain. They were necessary, bold, and risky. Many opposed them, many questioned them, but history has vindicated your vision. The India we see today—one of the fastest-growing economies in the world, a hub for global businesses, and a powerhouse of innovation—owes much of its success to the seeds you planted in those crucial years.

Leadership Without Noise

The hallmark of your leadership has always been your quiet demeanor and your ability to let actions speak louder than words. In an era where political leaders often rely on theatrics and grandstanding, you remained a figure of dignity, intellect, and measured decision-making.

As Prime Minister from 2004 to 2014, you once again steered India through complex challenges, including global financial crises, internal security threats, and the rapid evolution of global geopolitics. Your leadership was instrumental in ensuring economic stability, strengthening India's global standing, and advancing key social welfare programs. Initiatives like the Mahatma Gandhi National Rural Employment Guarantee Act (MGNREGA) and the Right to Information Act (RTI) empowered millions of Indians, ensuring greater transparency and economic security for the most vulnerable sections of society.

Yet, despite these achievements, your tenure was often met with criticism—not for inefficiency, but for your reserved approach to governance. Some mistook your silence for weakness, failing to see the immense strength it takes to lead with restraint and wisdom. But history will remember that true leadership is not about dominating headlines; it is about making decisions that stand the test of time.

A Personal Note of Gratitude

On a personal level, writing this book has been a journey of reflection and appreciation for the silent forces that drive change. In studying the progress of modern India, your name emerged time and again as a figure of immense influence, often understated but undeniably powerful.

Your resilience in the face of criticism, your ability to stay above political battles, and your unwavering commitment to India's development are qualities that I deeply admire. If there is one lesson that I hope readers take away from this book, it is that real revolutions do not always happen on the streets or in the headlines; sometimes, they happen in quiet offices, in policy papers, and in the decisions made by those who have the vision to see beyond the present.

Conclusion

Dr. Singh, this book is dedicated to you—not just as a tribute to your leadership, but as a recognition of the silent revolution you have led and continue to inspire. India stands stronger today because of your contributions, and no matter how history judges different eras of governance, one truth remains undeniable: your impact on this nation is profound and enduring.

Thank you for your service, your vision, and your unwavering belief in India's potential.

With deepest respect and gratitude,**Shivam**

Introduction

“**H**ow does Dr. Singh's journey inspire your views on leadership and governance?”

Chapter 1: The Quiet Architect of Change

India's modern history is dotted with towering personalities known for their charisma, fiery oratory, and public appeal. Amidst this gallery of leaders stands a quiet and unassuming figure—Dr. Manmohan Singh. Known as the architect of India's economic liberalisation, Dr. Singh's life and work embody resilience, intellect, and the power of understated leadership. This chapter explores his significance as a pivotal figure in India's transformation and introduces the themes that define his remarkable journey.

A Legacy of Transformation

When Dr. Manmohan Singh assumed the role of India's Finance Minister in 1991, the nation stood on the brink of economic collapse. Foreign reserves had dwindled to alarming levels, inflation was soaring, and the country's closed economy was struggling to keep pace with a rapidly globalising world. It was under these dire circumstances that Singh introduced sweeping economic reforms, dismantling decades of protectionism and setting India on the path to becoming one of the world's fastest-growing economies.

His tenure as Prime Minister from 2004 to 2014 saw India achieve significant milestones in economic growth, technological advancements, and social welfare. Yet, despite these achievements, Singh remained a polarising figure, celebrated by many for his intellect and integrity but criticised by others for his perceived reticence.

The Power of Silence

Dr. Singh's leadership style was markedly different from that of his predecessors and contemporaries. While many leaders relied on rhetoric and public demonstrations of power, Singh's approach was defined by quiet resolve and a steadfast focus on policy. His silence, often misunderstood as weakness, was in fact a reflection of his belief in substance over spectacle.

This unique style of leadership allowed him to navigate the turbulent waters of Indian politics, balancing coalition pressures, public expectations, and the complexities of governance. It also earned him respect as a leader who preferred action over words and intellect over theatrics.

Themes of Resilience, Intellect, and Leadership

Dr. Singh's journey from a small village in rural Punjab to the highest offices of academia, finance, and politics is a testament to his resilience. Despite facing numerous challenges—be it the trauma of Partition, the demands of an academic career abroad, or the scrutiny of public office—he remained committed to his vision of a stronger, more inclusive India.

His intellect, shaped by rigorous academic training at institutions like Cambridge and Oxford, became the foundation of his success. Singh's expertise in economics, coupled with his global outlook, enabled him to design policies that balanced growth with equity, earning him recognition as one of the world's leading economists.

As a leader, Singh demonstrated the power of humility and collaboration. Whether working under Prime Minister P.V. Narasimha Rao during the economic reforms or leading a coalition government as Prime Minister, his ability to build consensus and focus on long-term goals set him apart.

A Leader for the Times

Dr. Manmohan Singh's life and career represent a silent revolution in Indian leadership. At a time when political discourse often prioritised populism and showmanship, Singh's quiet determination and intellectual rig-or served as a powerful reminder of the potential of thoughtful governance. His journey, marked by personal sacrifices and professional triumphs, holds valuable lessons for current and future generations.

This book aims to delve into the complexities of Dr. Singh's life and work, exploring his humble beginnings, his transformative role in India's economic history, and his legacy as a leader who let his actions speak louder than words. As we journey through his story, we will uncover the essence of a man whose silence revolutionised a nation.

———◦———

"THE LEADER IS ONLY a facilitator, not a decision maker for others. The decisions should come from the collective wisdom of the people."

-Dr. Manmohan Singh

Part I: Humble Beginnings
Chapter 2: Roots in Rural Punjab

In the serene fields of Gah, a small village in the Punjab province of British India, a boy was born on September 26, 1932, who would go on to redefine India's economic and political landscape. Dr. Manmohan Singh's early life in this rural setting was marked by simplicity, hard work, and deep values that would shape his character and leadership style.

Life in Gah: A Rural Foundation

Gah, located in what is now Pakistan, was a quintessential Punjabi village. It lacked modern infrastructure but was rich in community spirit and cultural traditions. Singh's family was part of the Sikh minority in the region, living a modest but respectable life.

Manmohan was a quiet and studious child, often found reading under the shade of trees while other children played in the fields. The rhythm of rural life—marked by the sowing and harvesting of crops—instilled in him an appreciation for simplicity and perseverance.

His father, Gurmukhi Singh, worked as a trader, ensuring the family's basic needs were met. However, his mother, Amrit Kaur, passed away when he was very young, leaving a void that was filled by the care and guidance of his grandmother. This early loss imbued him with a sense of responsibility and maturity beyond his years.

The Partition: A Life-Changing Event

The Partition of 1947 was a watershed moment in the history of the Indian subcontinent, and for Manmohan Singh, it was a personal tragedy. The creation of India and Pakistan led to one of the largest mass migrations in human history, accompanied by widespread violence and upheaval.

Singh's family, like millions of others, was forced to leave their ancestral home in Gah and relocate to Amritsar in newly independent India. The trauma of displacement, coupled with the loss of their homeland, left a deep imprint on Singh's psyche. Witnessing the suffering of refugees and the horrors of communal violence further reinforced his belief in the importance of peace, tolerance, and coexistence.

Values Instilled During Childhood

Despite the hardships, Singh's upbringing was rooted in strong values. His family emphasised education, honesty, and humility—traits that would become hallmarks of his personality. His father encouraged him to pursue knowledge, often telling him that education was the only wealth that could never be taken away.

The teachings of Sikhism also played a pivotal role in shaping his character. The principles of selfless service, hard work, and humility resonated deeply with him, guiding his actions throughout his life.

The Seeds of Leadership

The challenges of his early life—the struggles of rural existence, the loss of his mother, and the upheaval of Partition—served as crucibles that forged Singh's resilience and empathy. His ability to remain calm under pressure and his quiet determination to succeed were evident even in these formative years.

Singh's academic potential was apparent early on. Encouraged by his family and teachers, he excelled in his studies, laying the foundation for a remarkable academic journey that would take him to some of the world's most prestigious institutions.

Reflections on Humble Beginnings

Manmohan Singh's childhood in Gah and the experiences of Partition were not just chapters in his life story—they were defining moments that shaped his worldview. The lessons of simplicity, perseverance, and empathy learned during these years remained with him as he navigated the complexities of economic reform and political leadership.

From the fields of Gah to the corridors of power in New Delhi, Singh's journey is a testament to the enduring power of humility and determination. As he often reflected, it was these humble beginnings that prepared him for the monumental challenges that lay ahead, giving him the strength to lead India through some of its most transformative years.

Chapter 3: The Scholar's Journey

D r. Manmohan Singh's life is a testament to the transformative power of education. Born into modest circumstances, his exceptional intellect and unrelenting dedication propelled him to academic heights few could imagine. This chapter delves into Singh's scholarly pursuits in India and abroad, and how his education shaped his economic philosophy and vision for India's future.

Early Academic Foundations

After resettling in Amritsar post-Partition, Singh joined Hindu College, where his brilliance began to shine. He excelled in economics, a subject that intrigued him for its ability to explain complex societal challenges. Recognising his potential, his teachers encouraged him to pursue higher studies, setting him on a path that would ultimately take him far beyond the classrooms of Punjab.

Singh graduated from Panjab University with top honours, earning a Bachelor's and then a Master's degree in Economics. His academic achievements earned him a scholarship to the University of Cambridge, an opportunity that would profoundly influence his intellectual and professional trajectory.

Cambridge: The Shaping of an Economist

Arriving at Cambridge in the early 1950s, Singh found himself in the company of some of the greatest minds in economics. He studied under influential economists like Joan Robinson and Nicholas Calder, whose progressive and analytical approaches to economic theory left a lasting impression on him.

Joan Robinson, in particular, played a pivotal role in shaping Singh's thinking. Her emphasis on addressing inequality and her critiques of traditional capitalist systems resonated deeply with him. Singh was drawn to the idea of using economic policies to promote social equity, a theme that would define his career.

Cambridge also exposed Singh to a global perspective. For a young man from rural Punjab, this was a transformative experience. He learned to see economic challenges not just as numbers on a ledger but as issues affecting real people, particularly those on the margins of society.

Doctoral Studies at Oxford

Singh's thirst for knowledge led him to pursue a DPhil in Economics at Nuffield College, Oxford. His doctoral thesis, *India's Export Trends and Prospects for Self-Sustained Growth*, examined the structural issues in India's trade policies and their impact on economic development.

In his thesis, Singh argued for liberalising trade policies and integrating India into the global economy, ideas that were ahead of their time in the context of post-independence India's focus on self-reliance. His work demonstrated a keen understanding of the challenges facing developing nations and offered practical solutions rooted in empirical research.

Forming His Economic Philosophy

Singh's academic journey at Cambridge and Oxford was instrumental in shaping his economic philosophy. He was influenced by Keynesian economics, which advocated for government intervention to stabilise economies, and by development economics, which emphasised the role of the state in addressing poverty and inequality.

At the same time, Singh recognised the limitations of over-reliance on state control, particularly in stifling innovation and efficiency. He envisioned a balanced approach—combining state-led initiatives with market-driven growth—that would later guide his landmark economic reforms.

Singh also developed a deep appreciation for the interconnectedness of global economies. His studies underscored the importance of trade, investment, and technological exchange in driving growth, themes that would feature prominently in his policymaking.

Mentors and Influences

Throughout his academic journey, Singh was fortunate to have mentors who recognised his potential and challenged him to think critically. Joan Robinson's progressive ideals, Nicholas Kaldor's analytical rig-or, and the intellectual environment at Cambridge and Oxford helped Singh develop a nuanced understanding of economics as both a science and a tool for societal change.

Additionally, Singh's exposure to the post-war economic reconstruction of Europe highlighted the transformative power of sound economic policies, further inspiring him to contribute to India's development.

Return to India: A Scholar with a Mission

Armed with world-class education and a deep sense of purpose, Singh returned to India in the late 1950s. He was not content to remain in academia, although he initially took up teaching positions at institutions like the Delhi School of Economics. He wanted to apply his knowledge to solve real-world problems and help build a prosperous and equitable India.

This chapter of Singh's life marks the beginning of his transition from a brilliant scholar to a visionary policymaker. His academic journey not only equipped him with the tools to understand India's challenges but also instilled in him the belief that economic policies could be a force for social good.

Chapter 4: The Economist Returns Home

After completing his doctoral studies at Oxford, Dr. Manmohan Singh returned to India in the early 1960s, equipped with advanced economic knowledge and a global perspective. The next phase of his life would see him transition from an academician to a practical economist, navigating the complex world of Indian policymaking while shaping the nation's economic future. His early career marked the beginning of a remarkable journey that would one day position him at the helm of India's economic transformation.

A Return to Teaching

Upon his return to India, Singh initially took up a teaching position at the Delhi School of Economics, where he continued to hone his academic skills while contributing to the education of the next generation of economists. His reputation as a brilliant scholar quickly spread, and he gained a following among students and academics alike. Despite his success in the classroom, Singh's ambitions extended far beyond academia. He wanted to contribute to India's economic development, particularly in a time when the country's economy was struggling to find its footing.

Entering the World of Policy

In the 1960s, India's economy was under the heavy influence of Nehruvian socialism, which emphasised state-led industrialisation and import substitution. However, by the 1970s, the inefficiencies of this system began to emerge, and India was grappling with issues such as sluggish growth, high inflation, and a widening fiscal deficit. Singh, with his deep understanding of global economic trends, began to realise that India needed a new approach.

In 1971, Singh took a step into the world of policymaking when he was appointed as the Chief Economist at the Planning Commission of India. His role here involved analysing the country's economic conditions and offering policy recommendations. He quickly established himself as a leading economist, capable of analysing complex economic data and translating it into actionable policy suggestions.

Singh's deep insights into India's challenges, particularly in the realms of trade, fiscal policy, and industrial growth, earned him respect within governmental circles. However, his next big step came when he was invited to work for the Indian government in an advisory capacity, leading to his collaboration with the Indian government on issues related to economic reforms.

Work at the World Bank

In 1972, Singh's expertise was recognised on the global stage when he was appointed as an economic advisor to the Reserve Bank of India (RBI). This was a pivotal moment in his career, as it allowed him to work closely with the country's central bank and contribute to shaping monetary policies that would drive India's growth.

A few years later, Singh's career took him abroad when he joined the World Bank as a senior economic advisor. Working with the global development institution exposed Singh to international best practices in economic planning and development. His work at the World Bank focused on the economics of poverty alleviation and development strategies for emerging economies, and it profoundly influenced his views on the importance of international cooperation and trade liberalisation.

His time at the World Bank broadened Singh's understanding of global markets, trade relations, and development economics, giving him the insight that would later be instrumental in guiding India's own economic liberalisation process. He observed how the most successful economies of the time had embraced open markets, deregulation, and international trade—ideas that he would later champion upon his return to India.

A Rising Star in Indian Economics

Upon returning to India, Singh's global experience and advanced economic knowledge quickly caught the attention of India's policymakers. In the 1980s, as the Indian economy continued to stagnate, Singh was appointed as the Economic Advisor to the Indian government, where he began playing an increasingly prominent role in shaping economic policy.

By the early 1990s, India was facing an acute balance of payments crisis. Foreign exchange reserves had dwindled to near-zero levels, inflation was soaring, and the government's ability to manage the economy was severely compromised. It was at this critical juncture that Dr. Singh was appointed as the Finance Minister of India in 1991 by Prime Minister P.V. Narasimha Rao. This marked a turning point in Singh's career and the trajectory of India's economic future.

The Path to Economic Reforms

As an economist, Singh had a clear vision: India needed to integrate into the global economy, move beyond protectionism, and embrace market-driven growth. His previous work with the World Bank and his understanding of global economic systems had prepared him for this moment. Singh knew that India could no longer afford to remain isolated from global trade, investment, and technology.

With the support of Prime Minister Rao, Singh began to devise and implement radical economic reforms that would reshape India's economy for generations to come. The reforms, which included liberalising trade, reducing tariffs, deregulating industries, and attracting foreign investment, marked the beginning of a new era in Indian economic history.

Legacy of His Early Work

Dr. Singh's return to India as an economist and his early work with the Planning Commission, Reserve Bank of India, and World Bank laid the foundation for his later success as the architect of India's economic liberalisation. His academic expertise, practical experience, and global outlook allowed him to navigate the complexities of economic policymaking and prepare India for the challenges of the 21st century.

His tenure as an economic advisor, and later as Finance Minister, was defined by a commitment to economic growth, social equity, and global integration. Singh's ability to synthesise his academic insights with the practical realities of India's economy would set the stage for the monumental reforms he would soon initiate, forever altering the country's economic landscape.

"While we have made significant progress, the fight against poverty and inequality remains a challenge. We must continue to focus on inclusive growth to ensure that the benefits of development reach everyone."

——Dr.Singh

Part II: The Architect of Economic Reform
Chapter 5: The Crisis of 1991

The year 1991 marked one of the most critical junctures in India's post-independence history. Facing an unprecedented economic crisis, the country stood at the edge of a precipice, with its economic survival in question. Amid this turmoil, Dr. Manmohan Singh was appointed as the Finance Minister of India. His leadership during this crisis would not only save the country from the brink of collapse but also set it on a path to becoming one of the world's fastest-growing economies. This chapter delves into the context of India's economic crisis in 1991 and how Dr. Singh's appointment as Finance Minister changed the course of India's economic history.

The Economic Crisis of 1991

India's economic problems had been building up for decades. For much of its post-independence history, India had followed a strategy of import substitution industrialisation, relying heavily on state control of industry and protectionist policies. These policies, combined with poor infrastructure, inefficiencies, and mounting corruption, had stunted economic growth and made the country highly dependent on imports. By the late 1980s, the economic conditions had worsened, and India was facing severe financial distress.

In the early 1990s, the crisis reached a tipping point. India's foreign exchange reserves had dwindled to just about $1 billion, enough to cover only a few weeks of imports. The country was staring at a balance of payments crisis, and the government was unable to service its external debt. The rupee was severely devalued, and inflation was skyrocketing.

In addition to the external financial pressures, India was also facing a domestic crisis of governance. The political landscape was unstable, with a fragile coalition government under Prime Minister Vishwanath Pratap Singh. The country was also grappling with rising social unrest and the aftermath of the liberalisation of the Soviet Union, which had altered the geopolitical landscape.

India was teetering on the edge of defaulting on its international debt obligations, which could have led to even more severe economic consequences. Faced with the possibility of national bankruptcy, there were calls for India to seek assistance from the International Monetary Fund (IMF), which would have meant submitting to stringent economic conditions and austerity measures.

THE ROLE OF DR. SINGH

In this moment of crisis, Dr. Manmohan Singh was appointed as Finance Minister in 1991 by Prime Minister P.V. Narasimha Rao. At the time, Singh was not a traditional politician but an economist of international renown, known for his deep understanding of economic theory and policy. His appointment was a strategic move by the Prime Minister, who recognised that India needed a visionary economist to guide it through this perilous moment.

Singh's reputation as a pragmatic and capable economist had already been established through his work at the Planning Commission, the Reserve Bank of India, and his time at the World Bank. However, the scale and urgency of the crisis were unprecedented. He was tasked with the monumental challenge of stabilising India's economy and laying the groundwork for future growth—all while working within the constraints of a politically volatile environment.

The Immediate Actions

Upon assuming office, Dr. Singh wasted no time in confronting the crisis head-on. His first priority was to stabilise the country's financial situation and restore international confidence in India's economy. One of his immediate actions was to approach the International Monetary Fund (IMF) for a loan, which provided India with much-needed financial breathing room.

Simultaneously, Singh's team worked to stabilise the currency, re-establish foreign exchange reserves, and bring inflation under control. His efforts included devaluing the rupee, a move that was highly controversial at the time but necessary to restore India's external competitiveness. The rupee's devaluation, along with several other reforms, signalled India's willingness to embrace market-driven policies, despite the country's historical hesitance towards such measures.

The Bold Economic Reforms

While stabilising the economy was an immediate concern, Dr. Singh and Prime Minister Narasimha Rao recognised that India's economic future required structural reforms that went beyond short term fixes. With a mandate to open up the economy, Singh took bold steps that would forever change India's economic trajectory.

The key reforms included:

1. **Economic Liberalisation**: Singh and his team began to dismantle the heavily protectionist trade regime, reducing tariffs and import quotas that had long shielded Indian industries from foreign competition. This marked the beginning of India's integration into the global economy, opening up the country to international trade and investment.

2. **Privatisation and Deregulation**: The government reduced its direct control over industries and began to privatise state-owned enterprises. This was a decisive break from the Nehruvian model of state-led development. Singh and his team recognised that for India to compete globally, it needed to unleash the potential of its private sector.

3. **Tax Reforms**: The Indian tax system was overburdened and inefficient. Singh introduced a series of tax reforms aimed at simplifying the system and improving compliance. These reforms would not only boost government revenue but also in-still confidence in both domestic and foreign investors.

4. **Financial Sector Reforms**: Singh's government restructured the financial sector, including reforms in banking and capital markets, to improve their efficiency and accessibility. This laid the groundwork for future growth in India's financial markets and allowed for greater foreign investment.

A Transformative Moment

The 1991 crisis was a defining moment in India's history. While the immediate reforms were harsh and controversial, they were essential for the long-term stability and growth of the country. Dr. Singh's ability to take decisive action under extreme pressure, despite the political risks, cemented his reputation as one of India's greatest economic leaders.

India's foreign exchange reserves stabilised, inflation was brought under control, and the economy slowly began to recover. These early reforms laid the foundation for the rapid economic growth that would follow in the years to come. By the end of the 1990s, India's economy was growing at an average rate of 6-7% annually, and the country had firmly established itself as a rising economic power on the global stage.

The Political and Personal Challenges

Despite the success of the economic reforms, Dr. Singh faced significant political opposition, both from within his party and the opposition. The economic reforms were seen by many as too drastic, and there were concerns that they would hurt the interests of certain sections of society. The opposition accused the government of betraying India's socialist ideals in favour of neoliberalism.

Singh, however, remained steadfast. His quiet resolve, humility, and technocratic approach enabled him to weather the storm of political criticism. He was unflinching in his belief that India's future depended on embracing a market-driven approach to economic growth.

Legacy of the Crisis of 1991

The economic crisis of 1991 was the moment that reshaped India's economic future. Dr. Singh's leadership not only helped India survive the immediate financial crisis but also set the country on a path of sustained economic growth. The reforms of 1991 were the beginning of a silent revolution that transformed India from a largely agrarian economy into one of the world's fastest-growing economies.

The lessons learned from the crisis of 1991 continue to influence India's economic policies today. Dr. Singh's calm leadership, his embrace of economic liberalisation, and his unwavering commitment to India's development remain central to his legacy as the architect of India's economic reforms.

Chapter 6: Economic Liberalisation: The Turning Point

In 1991, India was on the brink of economic collapse. The country's foreign exchange reserves had dwindled to just two weeks' worth of imports, inflation was soaring, and the fiscal deficit was out of control. It was a moment of crisis but also one of opportunity—an opportunity for profound change. Dr. Manmohan Singh, then appointed as the Finance Minister under Prime Minister P.V. Narasimha Rao, stood at the helm of this critical juncture in India's history. The economic liberalisation that followed would become known as the "1991 Reforms"—a turning point that fundamentally altered India's trajectory, not just in economic terms but also in its position on the global stage.

The Crisis of 1991: A Catalyst for Change

To understand the significance of the reforms, one must first grasp the gravity of the crisis. India had been operating under a highly controlled and protectionist economy since independence. A system of import substitution, high tariffs, and tight regulations dominated the landscape. By the late 1980s and early 1990s, the inefficiencies of this model were glaringly apparent. The country's growth had stagnated, and a series of external shocks exacerbated the situation: rising oil prices, a global recession, and political instability.

The trigger for India's economic crisis came in early 1991, when the country's foreign exchange reserves plummeted, leaving India with little more than a few days' worth of imports. In order to meet immediate financial obligations, India had to secure emergency loans from the International Monetary Fund (IMF). However, the IMF's condition for granting these loans was stark: India had to implement sweeping economic reforms. This would involve dismantling the existing economic structure, which had been in place for decades, and embracing market-oriented reforms that would expose India to global competition.

Dr. Singh's Vision for Reform

Dr. Manmohan Singh, a brilliant economist with training from prestigious institutions like Cambridge and Oxford, was the architect of these reforms.

He recognised that India's long-term survival required a shift from a closed, bureaucratic economy to an open, market-driven one. Despite his reputation as a quiet, reserved technocrat, Dr. Singh's policy vision was bold. His economic philosophy was deeply influenced by the belief that India's potential could only be unlocked by embracing globalisation and reducing the role of the state in economic matters.

The reforms he initiated were far-reaching and ambitious. The centrepiece of these reforms was the liberalisation of the Indian economy, which involved reducing trade barriers, deregulating industries, and encouraging foreign investment. These policies were designed not only to stabilise the economy but also to integrate India into the global economic system, making it more competitive and open to international opportunities.

Key Reforms Under Dr. Singh's Leadership

1. **Devaluation of the Rupee**
   One of the first major steps taken by Dr. Singh was the devaluation of the Indian rupee. The rupee had been artificially overvalued for years, a policy that had hurt Indian exports and drained the country's foreign exchange reserves. By allowing the rupee to depreciate, Dr. Singh aimed to make Indian exports more competitive on the global market and stimulate growth in export-oriented sectors such as textiles, software, and pharmaceuticals. The devaluation, while controversial, was a necessary step to restore balance in India's external accounts.

2. **Trade Liberalisation**
   India had long followed a protectionist economic model, with high tariffs and import restrictions designed to shield domestic industries from foreign competition. Under Dr. Singh, India significantly reduced tariffs and eased restrictions on imports. The government also began to encourage foreign direct investment (FDI) by creating a more attractive environment for international companies. The trade liberalisation measures were a game-changer, leading to an increase in foreign investment, technology transfers, and the growth of export sectors.

1. **Privatisation and Deregulation**

For decades, India's economy had been characterised by state control over key industries. Dr. Singh recognised that these state-run enterprises were inefficient and a drain on the public exchequer. As part of the 1991 reforms, he initiated a process of privatisation, selling off stakes in state-owned enterprises and encouraging private sector participation in previously government-dominated sectors. Along with privatisation, Dr. Singh pushed for deregulation, reducing the number of licenses and permits required to start and run businesses. These changes unleashed entrepreneurial energy and allowed the private sector to become the primary driver of economic growth.

2. **Financial Sector Reforms**

   The financial sector in India had been underdeveloped and rigid, with state-run banks dominating the landscape. Dr. Singh's reforms sought to modernise the sector by introducing measures to increase transparency, competition, and efficiency. The Reserve Bank of India (RBI) was given greater autonomy, and interest rates were liberalised. At the same time, the government began to encourage the development of private banks and non-bank financial institutions, which helped increase access to credit and improve the overall health of the financial system.

3. **Tax Reforms**

   India's tax system prior to 1991 was complex and riddled with loopholes. High tax rates, combined with poor compliance, had created an inefficient and inequitable tax regime. Dr. Singh's reforms included simplifying the tax structure, reducing corporate tax rates, and broadening the tax base. These changes were aimed at improving revenue collection, encouraging investment, and reducing the burden on businesses and individuals. The introduction of the Goods and Services Tax (GST) in the years that followed can be seen as an extension of these tax reforms.

The Immediate Impact: Stabilisation and Growth

While the reforms were initially met with skepticism and resistance, they soon began to yield results. India's foreign exchange reserves were replenished, inflation moderated, and the economy gradually stabilised. The economic liberalisation measures also paved the way for faster growth. By the mid-1990s, India's GDP growth rate had accelerated to over 6% annually, a significant improvement from the stagnation of the preceding decades.

One of the most striking results of the 1991 reforms was the growth of India's export sectors. The liberalisation of trade and the competitive exchange rate helped Indian companies expand their presence in global markets. The software and IT services industries, in particular, saw tremendous growth, with companies like Infosys, Wipro, and Tata Consultancy Services emerging as global players. India's information technology boom, which would come to define its 21st-century economic rise, was set into motion by the policy shifts of 1991.

Long-term Impacts: India's Transformation into a Global Player

The liberalisation of the Indian economy in 1991 laid the foundation for India's transformation into one of the world's fastest-growing economies. The immediate results—stabilisation of the economy, rising exports, and increasing foreign investment—were just the beginning. In the decades that followed, India's economic growth would become increasingly driven by the private sector, with new industries emerging, technology advancements accelerating, and infrastructure development feeling expansion.

By the 2000s, India was not only growing rapidly but was also seen as a critical player on the global stage. Its economic power was reflected in its rising stature as a global economic and technological hub. The policies initiated by Dr. Singh in 1991, despite the short-term challenges they posed, positioned India for a future of unprecedented growth.

Chapter 7: Balancing Politics and Economics

As India's Finance Minister during the 1991 economic crisis, Dr. Manmohan Singh faced a monumental challenge. While he was entrusted with the responsibility of guiding the country through an economic storm, he also had to navigate the complex political landscape that often clashed with the vision for reforms he had. The reforms he introduced were not only a radical departure from the old system but also required significant political consensus to succeed.

The environment in which these economic policies were introduced was one of intense political volatility. India's political system was characterised by a fragile coalition of parties, each with their own interests, and by political resistance to change. Economic reforms were often seen by some political factions as a threat to their entrenched power. Dr. Singh, a man of quiet demean-or and few words, had to balance his economic vision with the realities of coalition politics and public sentiment. This chapter explores the challenges he faced in balancing economics and politics and the dynamic relationship between Dr. Singh and Prime Minister P.V. Narasimha Rao, which played a crucial role in pushing through these reforms.

Challenges of Implementing Reforms in a Politically Volatile Environment

Implementing economic reforms in India in 1991 was a delicate operation, akin to performing surgery on a patient who was already in critical condition. The country's economic crisis, triggered by a sharp decline in foreign exchange reserves, high inflation, and rising external debt, made immediate reforms necessary. However, it was the political environment that complicated the implementation of these reforms.

India's political scene in the early 1990s was fraught with challenges. The Congress party, which had long been the dominant force in Indian politics, was experiencing internal divisions. The party had just seen a massive defeat in the 1989 general elections, and by 1991, it had only a slim majority in the Lok Sabha. This meant that Dr. Singh had to garner support not only from his own party but also from smaller coalition partners to push through his economic agenda.

The 1991 reforms, which involved market liberalisation, privatisation of state-owned industries, and opening up India to foreign investments, were radical for a nation that had long been governed by socialist policies. Such reforms threatened the interests of various political constituencies, from labor unions to bureaucrats to the public sector lobby. The political opposition was also keen to exploit any potential vulnerabilities in the reforms, seeing them as a path to undermine the ruling government.

Despite these pressures, Dr. Singh remained steadfast. He had the intellectual clarity to argue the case for economic liberalisation, but more importantly, he recognised that the success of these reforms would require careful political management. The ability to keep the political establishment aligned with his economic vision was crucial, and for that, he had to convince both the ruling Congress party and its coalition partners that the reforms were in the country's long-term interest.

The Role of P.V. Narasimha Rao: A Unique Partnership

While Dr. Singh was the architect of India's economic reforms, it was Prime Minister P.V. Narasimha Rao who played a pivotal role in facilitating their political success. Rao, who became Prime Minister in 1991, was a seasoned politician with an acute understanding of Indian politics and an exceptional ability to navigate its complexities. The relationship between Dr. Singh and Rao was one of mutual respect and trust, with each man complementing the other's strengths.

Narasimha Rao, despite having been known for his pragmatic and sometimes cautious approach, understood the urgency of the situation. He was aware that the economic reforms proposed by Dr. Singh were necessary to prevent India from spiralling into a prolonged crisis. Rao was also politically astute enough to recognise that the reforms would be unpopular with certain sections of society, particularly labor unions, which were likely to resist privatisation, and the industrialists, who had grown accustomed to the protectionist policies of the past.

One of Rao's most important contributions was his ability to shield Dr. Singh from some of the more difficult political pressures. As a skilled political strategist, Rao ensured that Singh could focus on the economic reforms while he dealt with the political fallout. He provided the political cover needed to manage opposition from within and outside the Congress party. Rao also worked to maintain the support of coalition partners, some of whom were wary of the liberalisation process. It was a unique collaboration—while Dr. Singh remained the intellectual driving force behind the reforms, Rao used his political acumen to ensure their successful passage through Parliament.

Together, the duo made a formidable team. Singh brought to the table his technical expertise and vision, while Rao brought his political wisdom and ability to communicate the necessity of reforms to the broader public. They both understood that the success of the reforms required not only economic changes but also careful political messaging and consensus-building.

Public and Political Resistance

Despite their best efforts, the road to economic liberalisation was not without its obstacles. Dr. Singh faced significant resistance from both the political establishment and certain sections of the public. Opposition parties criticised the reforms as pro-business and anti-poor. The trade unions were unhappy with the privatisation of state-owned enterprises, fearing it would lead to job losses. The political left, which had traditionally supported socialist policies, vehemently opposed the liberalisation agenda, viewing it as a betrayal of India's independence-era ideals of self-reliance.

In the midst of this, Dr. Singh had to maintain a delicate balance—pushing for reforms while also managing the concerns of the political and economic stakeholders. His calm, understated demean-or stood in sharp contrast to the fiery rhetoric of many of his critics, but it was precisely this silence that gave him the moral authority to carry out the necessary changes. He knew that true leadership often meant taking difficult decisions, even in the face of adversity.

One of the significant hurdles Singh faced was managing the political fallout from the devaluation of the rupee and the opening up of India's economy to foreign competition. Both moves were seen as drastic measures that would have long-term implications for the Indian middle class, which was apprehensive about the effects of globalisation. At the same time, Singh had to contend with the domestic industrialists who had grown accustomed to a protectionist environment and were now worried about the opening of markets to foreign competition.

Strategic Leadership: The Way Forward

Dr. Singh's political savvy came to the fore when he made a strategic decision to frame the reforms not just as a solution to an economic crisis, but as a pathway to India's modernisation and global integration. By focusing on the long-term benefits—such as increased foreign investment, faster economic growth, and job creation—Singh and Rao were able to gain broader support for the reforms.

In addition to addressing immediate political concerns, Dr. Singh also understood that India's economic reforms would require strong and sustained leadership. This meant working on the ground to gain consensus from various political factions and economic sectors. He also made efforts to ensure that the benefits of liberalisation were distributed more equitably, launching several programs aimed at rural development, poverty alleviation, and infrastructure improvement.

Conclusion: A Legacy of Balance

Dr. Singh's ability to balance economics and politics, to keep his vision intact while navigating the complexities of coalition politics, was a defining feature of his leadership. His relationship with Prime Minister Narasimha Rao was crucial in ensuring the success of India's economic transformation. Together, they were able to push through policies that, despite initial opposition, paved the way for India's rise as a global economic power.

The lessons of 1991—the importance of political strategy in enacting economic reforms, the need for political consensus, and the necessity of visionary leadership in times of crisis—remain relevant even today. As India faces new challenges in the 21st century, the balancing act that Dr. Singh and Narasimha Rao performed offers valuable insights into how political leadership can shape a nation's economic future.

"The highest calling in life is to serve the people. Public service is a responsibility and a privilege."
—Dr. Singh

Part III: Political Leadership
Chapter 8: Reluctant Politician

Dr. Manmohan Singh's journey into politics was anything but conventional. Unlike many of his contemporaries, who entered the political arena driven by ambition and a desire for power, Dr. Singh was thrust into politics by necessity. His rise from a scholar and economist to one of the most influential political leaders in India was marked by reluctance, humility, and a quiet sense of duty. This chapter explores Dr. Singh's transition from a technocrat to a politician, his entry into Parliament, and his growth within the Congress party.

From Economist to Politician: A Reluctant Shift

Dr. Manmohan Singh's primary identity, throughout his early career, was that of an economist. He was deeply entrenched in his work, focused on economic research, and passionately dedicated to India's development through policy and analysis. His expertise in the field of economics earned him respect in international circles, particularly during his time at the World Bank and his work in various government roles. Singh had always preferred the academic and policy-driven environment to the cutthroat world of politics. His professional life had been about quiet intellectual rig-or rather than the public spotlight.

However, the economic crisis of 1991 forced Singh into the political arena. As India teetered on the edge of economic collapse, it became clear that a new direction was needed, and Dr. Singh's economic brilliance was recognised as the solution. Prime Minister P.V. Narasimha Rao, understanding the gravity of the situation, invited Singh to become the Finance Minister. Singh was initially reluctant to take on such a high-profile role. He was hesitant about leaving the world of economics for the often chaotic and controversial sphere of politics. Nonetheless, recognising the dire state of the nation's economy and feeling a sense of national responsibility, he agreed to serve in this unprecedented role.

Singh's entry into politics was not driven by ambition, but by an understanding that his expertise could help steer the nation out of its economic crisis. His approach was marked by his quiet determination and a sense of duty to the nation's future. For Dr. Singh, politics was not about personal gain or public recognition—it was about contributing to the greater good of the country, and in this, he was steadfast.

The Call to Parliament: Entering the Political Arena

Dr. Singh's appointment as Finance Minister was a pivotal moment in Indian politics. Although he was a senior economist with an international reputation, his lack of political experience made his entry into the Cabinet controversial. He was not a member of Parliament at the time, which was highly unusual for someone appointed to such a significant role. The move generated considerable discussion and skepticism among both politicians and the public.

In the eyes of many, Dr. Singh was an outsider in the political landscape. His intellectual and technocratic background contrasted sharply with the traditional political figures who dominated the Indian political scene. His first major hurdle was not just the economic reforms he had to implement, but also establishing his credibility within the highly politicised world of Indian governance.

To overcome this, Dr. Singh entered Parliament in 1999, after he was nominated to the Rajya Sabha (the Upper House of Parliament) by the Congress party. His presence in Parliament, however, did not immediately alter the perception of him as an outsider. The political world was still wary of him, seeing him as an economist who lacked the political instincts necessary to navigate India's turbulent political waters.

Growth Within the Congress Party

Although Singh's relationship with the Congress party was somewhat peripheral at first, it gradually deepened. His loyalty to the party, and his commitment to its goals, eventually allowed him to gain the trust of its leadership. This was not an easy feat. The Congress party, especially under the leadership of Sonia Gandhi, had its own entrenched power dynamics. Singh's quiet and unassuming nature, as well as his reserved approach to political drama, initially made it hard for him to break through.

Singh's role in the 1991 economic reforms, however, became a defining feature of his relationship with the Congress party. He was seen as a key player in the party's renewed credibility in the years following the economic liberalisation. His reforms made India's economy more competitive globally, and the success of these policies solidified his importance within the Congress party. Though he was not always the most visible political figure in the party, his intellectual leadership and deep commitment to India's development made him an indispensable member of the political establishment.

Dr. Singh's ascension within the Congress party also stemmed from his ability to remain above the political fray. He did not engage in power struggles, nor did he use populist tactics to appeal to the masses. His leadership style was defined by integrity, humility, and a focus on governance rather than political theatrics. These qualities earned him respect within Congress, and over time, he became the party's most trusted figure for economic policy and governance.

Becoming the Prime Minister: A Reluctant Leader

Dr. Singh's ultimate rise to the position of Prime Minister in 2004 was a culmination of his years of service to the nation, both in economics and in politics. However, even then, it was not a position he sought out. The Congress party, after winning the general elections of 2004, faced the challenge of selecting a leader. Sonia Gandhi, the Congress president at the time, was initially set to become the Prime Minister, but political opposition and public resistance to her foreign-born status led to her decision to decline the role.

In a remarkable turn of events, Sonia Gandhi proposed Dr. Singh's name for the position of Prime Minister. His reputation as a technocrat and a leader who had steered India through an economic transformation made him an ideal candidate. His humility and reluctance to engage in power politics also made him a figure who was trusted to be impartial and focused on the country's progress rather than personal political ambitions.

Dr. Singh's appointment as Prime Minister was, in many ways, a validation of his contributions to India's development. Yet, it was also a reflection of the trust that the Congress party and the Indian people placed in him. Though he had initially shied away from politics, Singh's leadership during his two terms as Prime Minister proved that he was not only capable of managing complex economic challenges but also of steering India through the intricacies of domestic and international political issues.

Chapter 9: The Prime Minister's Chair

Dr. Manmohan Singh's appointment as the Prime Minister of India in 2004 marked a significant moment in both his personal career and the history of Indian politics. After decades of service as an economist and technocrat, Singh was catapulted into the highest office in the land—not by ambition, but by circumstance and a sense of duty. His tenure as Prime Minister was characterised by both extraordinary achievements and considerable challenges, and his leadership style was as unconventional as his journey to the office. In this chapter, we explore Dr. Singh's appointment as Prime Minister, the public perception of his leadership, and his relationship with the Gandhi family, particularly Sonia Gandhi, whose influence played a critical role in his rise to the top.

The Appointment: A Moment of National Significance

The 2004 Indian general elections were a surprise to many. The ruling Bharathiya Janta Party (BJP), led by Prime Minister Atal Bihari Vajpayee, was expected to retain power, but the electorate's verdict defied predictions. The Congress party, led by Sonia Gandhi, secured a victory, but its leaders were faced with a dilemma: who would be the Prime Minister?

Sonia Gandhi, despite being the Congress president and leading the party to victory, chose not to assume the role of Prime Minister. Her decision was motivated by multiple factors, not least the intense opposition to her foreign-born status, particularly from Hindu nationalist factions and the BJP. After months of speculation and political negotiation, Sonia Gandhi made the surprising announcement that Dr. Manmohan Singh, a respected economist and her trusted ally, would be the Congress candidate for Prime Minister.

Singh's appointment was not just a personal milestone—it was also a defining moment for Indian politics. Here was a man of intellectual brilliance, a non-political figure, chosen to lead the world's largest democracy at a time of complex national and international challenges. While his name was already associated with the success of India's economic reforms, few expected him to take on the political mantle of Prime Minister. Yet, his appointment demonstrated the Congress party's faith in his integrity and capabilities, as well as the party's broader vision for a government focused on governance rather than political theatrics.

Public Perception: The Silent Leader

Dr. Manmohan Singh was, by nature, a quiet and reserved individual. Throughout his career, he had been more known for his intellect and policy acumen than for his public speaking or political posturing. When he assumed the Prime Minister's office, this reserved nature led to mixed public perceptions. On one hand, Singh's calm demeanour and absence of the typical political bravado helped him maintain an image of integrity and seriousness. He was seen as a man who would work for the nation's betterment rather than engage in political theatrics. For many, his understated leadership style was a refreshing contrast to the often divisive rhetoric of his predecessors.

However, this quiet demeanour also led to criticism, particularly from political opponents. Some felt that Singh lacked the charisma and assertiveness needed to lead a country as complex and diverse as India. His reserved nature was often misinterpreted as weakness or indecisiveness. In a political landscape that valued bold speeches and decisive action, Singh's preference for quiet diplomacy and pragmatic policy-making was at times seen as a liability.

Additionally, his leadership during his first tenure was frequently scrutinised by the media, which often portrayed him as a "puppet" Prime Minister under the influence of Sonia Gandhi. While this portrayal was largely unfair, it highlighted the challenges Singh faced in asserting his authority within the political structure. Despite his impressive credentials and decades of service, the fact that he was not seen as a political figure—more as a technocrat with little desire for power—became a point of contention.

The Relationship with the Gandhi Family

Dr. Manmohan Singh's relationship with Sonia Gandhi, and by extension the Gandhi family, was one of mutual respect and trust. Sonia Gandhi, after the unexpected victory in 2004, turned to Singh not only because of his economic expertise but also because of his unblemished reputation for integrity and his ability to navigate complex political scenarios. She recognised his intellectual prowess and acknowledged that he was the best person to steer the country during a period of growth and transformation.

Singh's relationship with Sonia Gandhi was built on a foundation of loyalty and gratitude. Singh had been brought into politics and given key roles by the

Gandhi family, particularly during the challenging years of economic reforms in the early 1990s. By 2004, he had become an essential part of the Congress party's leadership. The political alliance between Singh and the Gandhi family was crucial in maintaining the stability of the United Progressive Alliance (UPA), a coalition of parties that supported his government.

Despite the collaboration, there were tensions, particularly regarding the perception that Dr. Singh, though Prime Minister, had limited autonomy in decision-making. Many in the political establishment speculated about the nature of his influence within the government, especially given Sonia Gandhi's substantial role as Congress president. Critics often suggested that Dr. Singh was more of a technocrat than a traditional leader, and that his decisions were shaped by the political considerations of the Congress party rather than his own independent leadership.

However, those who knew Dr. Singh understood that his relationship with Sonia Gandhi was one of mutual respect and collaboration. Singh was not a "puppet" leader, as some detractors suggested; rather, he was a man who believed in the collective wisdom of the Congress party and its leaders, working within the framework of cooperation and compromise. He respected Sonia Gandhi's political insight and leadership, and in turn, she respected his intellect and principled leadership.

Navigating Coalition Politics

As Prime Minister of a coalition government, Singh had to navigate the complex web of Indian coalition politics, which was fraught with competing interests, regional pressures, and demands for policy changes. His leadership was a balancing act between ensuring that the government remained stable while managing the expectations of various coalition partners.

Unlike many other political leaders, Singh did not seek to dominate the political conversation or force his agenda through without compromise. Instead, he focused on creating a stable environment for policymaking, often working behind the scenes to build consensus. His low-key style of leadership was, at times, a disadvantage in a system where politicians often rely on personal charisma and public displays of power. However, his pragmatic approach ensured that the country was able to move forward on critical issues like economic development, poverty alleviation, and foreign relations.

Chapter 10: India's Economic and Technological Surge

Dr. Manmohan Singh's tenure as Prime Minister was a transformative period for India. From 2004 to 2014, India experienced remarkable economic growth, driven by a combination of factors including the IT boom, infrastructure development, and deeper integration into the global economy. Singh's leadership was instrumental in positioning India as a rising global economic power, steering the country through a rapidly changing world and leveraging India's inherent strengths. This chapter explores India's economic and technological surge during Dr. Singh's time in office and his role in navigating the complexities of globalisation.

The IT Boom: A New Era for India

One of the most defining features of India's economic growth during Dr. Singh's tenure was the unprecedented boom in the information technology (IT) and services sector. Building on the foundations laid in the 1990s, the IT industry flourished in the early 2000s, and India became a hub for global outsourcing, software development, and IT-enabled services. Cities like Bangalore, Hyderabad, and Pune emerged as global centres for IT innovation and outsourcing, creating millions of jobs and establishing India as an essential player in the global economy.

Under Singh's leadership, the Indian government continued to support the IT sector with policies designed to encourage foreign investment, improve infrastructure, and promote skill development. The advent of affordable internet access and the proliferation of mobile technology further furled the IT boom, helping India tap into global markets, particularly in the United States and Europe. The Indian IT industry's success was not only a boon for the economy but also helped shift the global perception of India from a country of poverty and underdevelopment to one of modernity and innovation.

The IT revolution provided a platform for millions of young professionals to make a mark on the global stage. India's burgeoning middle class benefited from the boom, and cities once considered backwaters became cosmopolitan hubs. The digital transformation initiated in these years laid the groundwork for India's role in the Fourth Industrial Revolution, making the IT sector one of the cornerstones of India's economic future.

Infrastructure Development: Bridging Gaps and Building Foundations

Alongside the IT sector's rapid expansion, Dr. Singh's government made significant strides in addressing the country's infrastructure deficit. For India to sustain its high rates of economic growth, the government recognised the need for better roads, railways, ports, airports, and power generation. Under Singh, there was a concerted effort to modernise India's infrastructure to support both the growth of its domestic economy and its position in the global supply chain.

One of the most ambitious initiatives during Singh's tenure was the National Highway Development Project (NHDP), which sought to create a network of modern highways that would link cities and states across India. These highways not only facilitated smoother transportation and trade but also helped reduce logistical costs, improving the overall competitiveness of Indian businesses.

Simultaneously, India made substantial investments in its power sector, including expanding electricity generation capacity, particularly from renewable sources. The country began to take steps toward addressing its energy challenges, which had long hindered industrial growth. Urbanisation also saw a boost, with the expansion of urban infrastructure, housing projects, and better public transport systems in cities like Delhi, Mumbai, and Bangalore.

While there were still significant challenges in rural infrastructure development, the efforts made in these areas during Singh's tenure laid the groundwork for future growth. The improved infrastructure helped attract foreign investments, boost domestic production, and enable India to integrate into global trade networks more effectively.

Globalisation and India's Economic Integration

Perhaps one of the most significant aspects of Dr. Singh's economic policy was his focus on globalisation and positioning India as a global economic player. Building on the liberalisation efforts of the early 1990s, Singh sought to deepen India's integration with the global economy. India, once a protectionist economy with limited foreign trade and investment, embraced a more open and market-oriented approach during his tenure.

Under Singh's leadership, India entered into several key trade agreements and strengthened its diplomatic ties with major economic powers, particularly the United States, the European Union, and the emerging economies of Asia. One of the most notable achievements in this regard was the nuclear deal with the United States in 2008. This landmark agreement allowed India to access civilian nuclear technology and was seen as a major step in solidifying India's position as a global power.

The government also pushed for the liberalisation of the financial sector, allowing foreign direct investment (FDI) in multiple sectors such as retail, insurance, and defence. FDI inflows surged during Singh's tenure, particularly in the fields of manufacturing, telecom, and retail. Singh's policies also emphasised the importance of creating a stable macroeconomic environment, including maintaining low inflation and ensuring fiscal discipline, which helped build investor confidence in India.

Additionally, Singh's government worked to modernise India's financial markets, paving the way for greater participation in global capital markets. The economic reforms of the early 2000s helped to position India as an attractive destination for foreign investment, and by the time he left office in 2014, India was firmly integrated into the global economic order.

The Challenges of Sustaining Growth

While India's economic surge during Dr. Singh's tenure was impressive, it was not without challenges. The global financial crisis of 2008 tested India's economic resilience. While India's economy was less affected than many others, the crisis did lead to a slowdown in growth and highlighted the vulnerabilities in the global economic system.

Dr. Singh's government had to navigate these challenges carefully, ensuring that India's growth remained steady in the face of global uncertainty. At the same time, inflationary pressures, particularly on food prices, became a concern for the government, and the rupee came under pressure in the global markets.

Despite these challenges, Dr. Singh's leadership helped India weather the storm. The country's growing economic clout, combined with its young population and technological prowess, kept India on a path of growth. India's emerging middle class continued to fuel domestic consumption, which acted as a buffer against global economic shocks.

India as a Global Economic Power

By the time Dr. Singh left office in 2014, India had firmly established itself as a rising global economic power. The country's GDP growth had consistently outpaced that of many developed nations, and India was on track to become one of the world's largest economies in the coming decades. The country's global standing was enhanced by its significant role in international forums such as the

G20, BRICS, and the World Trade Organisation (WTO). Singh's government also made strategic investments in India's foreign policy, emphasising economic diplomacy and strengthening India's relationships with key global players.

The growth in India's service and technology sectors, alongside its expanding manufacturing base, meant that the country was no longer seen merely as a back office for the world's major economies but as a vibrant, competitive player on the global stage. Dr. Singh's policies helped transform India's economic outlook, positioning the nation for the future challenges and opportunities of the 21st century.

Chapter 11: Key Policy Achievements

Dr. Manmohan Singh's time as Prime Minister was marked by several landmark policy achievements that had a profound and lasting impact on India's social, economic, and political landscape. While his economic reforms were groundbreaking, his government also focused on enhancing social welfare and addressing long-standing disparities within the country. This chapter examines some of the key policies introduced during his tenure, including the Mahatma Gandhi National Rural Employment Guarantee Act (MGNREGA), the Right to Information (RTI) Act, and the historic Indo-US nuclear deal. These initiatives reflected Singh's commitment to both economic modernisation and inclusive growth.

MGNREGA: Empowering Rural India

One of Dr. Singh's most significant contributions to rural development was the introduction of the Mahatma Gandhi National Rural Employment Guarantee Act (MGNREGA) in 2005. The scheme aimed to alleviate rural poverty by guaranteeing 100 days of wage employment per year to every rural household whose adult members were willing to do unskilled manual labor. It was designed to improve the livelihood security of rural populations by providing a social safety net and creating rural infrastructure.

MGNREGA represented a shift in India's approach to rural welfare, moving away from traditional top-down poverty alleviation programs and giving people the means to earn a living. The program not only provided employment but also contributed to rural development through the construction of roads, ponds, irrigation systems, and other infrastructure that benefited local communities. Over time, MGNREGA became one of the world's largest public employment programs, reaching millions of households across India.

However, the scheme also faced challenges, including concerns about corruption, delays in payments, and underutilisation in some areas. Despite these issues, MGNREGA's impact on rural India cannot be underestimated, as it contributed to reducing poverty and empowering marginalised communities.

Right to Information (RTI): Promoting Transparency and Accountability

Another key achievement of Dr. Singh's government was the passage of the Right to Information (RTI) Act in 2005. The RTI Act was a revolutionary step towards enhancing transparency and accountability in the functioning of government institutions. By empowering citizens with the right to access government records and information, the RTI Act provided a powerful tool to fight corruption and improve governance.

The law allowed citizens to seek information about government decisions, expenditures, and policies, which had previously been shrouded in secrecy. RTI played a pivotal role in uncovering cases of inefficiency, corruption, and misuse of power in both the central and state governments. It also empowered civil society organisations, journalists, and activists to hold government institutions accountable, thus strengthening India's democratic fabric.

While the RTI Act has been widely lauded as one of the most significant achievements of Dr. Singh's government, it has also faced challenges, particularly from bureaucratic resistance and attempts to limit its scope. Nonetheless, the RTI Act has had a lasting impact on Indian society, contributing to greater civic engagement and a more transparent political system.

Indo-US Nuclear Deal: A Historic Diplomatic Achievement

One of the most contentious but significant policy decisions of Dr. Singh's tenure was the Indo-US nuclear deal, finalised in 2008. The deal marked a major shift in India's foreign policy and its relationship with the United States. It allowed India to access civilian nuclear technology and materials, which were previously restricted due to the country's nuclear weapons program and non-signatory status to the Nuclear Non-Proliferation Treaty (NPT).

The nuclear deal was a diplomatic breakthrough for India. It marked the end of India's international isolation on the nuclear front and singled its emergence as a global player. The deal also had significant strategic and economic implications, as it opened up the possibility of increased energy security for India and bolstered its position in global geopolitics. Singh's government worked hard to secure international support for the deal, navigating complex diplomatic negotiations and domestic opposition.

The nuclear deal also had significant domestic implications, as it faced criticism from several political parties and sections of the public, who feared that it would compromise India's sovereignty and weaken its stance on nuclear disarmament. Despite the controversy, the deal passed and was seen as a major victory for Dr. Singh's foreign policy vision, enhancing India's ties with the United States and positioning the country as a key player in the global nuclear order.

Rural Development and Social Welfare: A Focus on Inclusivity

Throughout his tenure, Dr. Singh's government emphasised inclusive growth, particularly in addressing rural development and the welfare of marginalised communities. In addition to MGNREGA, the government launched several programs aimed at improving healthcare, education, and infrastructure in rural areas.

The Pradhan Mantri Gram Sadak Yojana (PMGSY), for example, was another important initiative focused on rural infrastructure. The scheme aimed to provide all-weather roads to rural areas, facilitating better connectivity, trade, and access to services like healthcare and education. Additionally, programs like the National Rural Health Mission (NRHM) and the National Rural Livelihood Mission (NRLM) aimed to improve health outcomes and create livelihood opportunities in rural India.

Dr. Singh also focused on improving social welfare schemes such as the National Food Security Act (NFSA), which sought to ensure food security for vulnerable sections of society by providing subsidised food grains. The government's focus on rural development and social welfare was a key part of Singh's vision for inclusive growth, ensuring that the benefits of India's economic rise reached all sections of society.

Chapter 12: Challenges in Leadership

While Dr. Manmohan Singh's tenure was marked by several achievements, it was also a period of immense political and leadership challenges. From navigating the complexities of coalition politics to facing allegations of corruption, Singh's leadership was constantly tested. This chapter explores the obstacles he encountered, the difficulties he faced in maintaining political stability, and the controversies that surrounded his government, particularly in its second term.

Navigating Coalition Politics and Opposition

Dr. Singh's government was a coalition government, which meant that he had to contend with the intricacies of balancing multiple political interests. The United Progressive Alliance (UPA), led by the Congress party, included several regional parties with varying agendas, which often created tensions in policymaking and governance. While the coalition model allowed for a broad representation of interests, it also meant that Singh had to negotiate and compromise with his allies regularly.

The biggest challenge came during UPA-II, after the 2009 general elections, when the government faced an increasingly fragmented political environment. Singh's leadership was often constrained by the demands of coalition partners, who sought to influence key decisions and policies. His commitment to consensus-building sometimes led to delays in implementing reforms, and certain important policy measures were watered down or abandoned due to political pressures.

Moreover, Singh's leadership was often overshadowed by the prominence of the Gandhi family, particularly Sonia Gandhi, who was the UPA chairperson. Critics argued that Dr. Singh's position as Prime Minister was more ceremonial and that real power lay with the Congress President. Singh's quiet, non-confrontational style of governance, while effective in some ways, also contributed to perceptions of indecisiveness and a lack of political authority.

Controversies and Criticisms: Corruption Scandals During UPA-II

In the second term of his tenure, Dr. Singh's government was embroiled in several corruption scandals that tarnished its reputation. The most significant of these was the 2G spectrum scandal, which alleged that government officials and politicians had underpriced spectrum licenses, leading to a loss of billions of dollars in government revenue. The scandal rocked the government and led to public outrage, putting Singh's administration on the defensive.

Other scandals, such as the Commonwealth Games corruption scandal and the coal allocation scam (known as Coalgate), also drew significant criticism. While Singh personally remained untainted by allegations of corruption, these scandals eroded public trust in his government. Critics accused him of being unable or unwilling to take decisive action against corruption within his own party and government.

Singh faced significant criticism for his passive leadership during these scandals. While he was seen as a man of integrity, his inability to effectively tackle corruption and take swift action against those involved contributed to the perception of a weak leadership. This period of corruption scandals and political turbulence marked a contrast to the earlier years of his tenure, when he was lauded for his economic policies and governance.

"Our aim was to free India from the shackles of economic stagnation and make it self-reliant and resilient in the global economy."

Dr. Manmohan Singh.

Part IV: The Man Behind the Leader
Chapter 13: The Personal Life of Manmohan Singh

Dr. Manmohan Singh's personal life offers valuable insights into the values and principles that shaped his leadership. While his public life as an economist and politician garnered much attention, it is his quiet, private demean-or and strong familial bonds that defined him as an individual. His marriage to Gursharan Kaur, whom he met during his time at Cambridge, was a cornerstone of his personal life. Their enduring relationship exemplified the deep respect, love, and support they shared, a stark contrast to the political world of intrigue and power struggles that he navigated in his professional career.

Gursharan Kaur, a devoted and accomplished woman in her own right, was an integral part of Dr. Singh's life, providing him with the stability and emotional support needed to carry out his demanding responsibilities. Despite being thrust into the political limelight, Dr. Singh's family life remained private, with his wife and daughters often staying out of the media's spotlight. His two daughters, Daman Singh and Amrit Singh, grew up in an environment where academic excellence, discipline, and values were paramount. These familial relationships, grounded in humility and strong ethical principles, served as a grounding force for Dr. Singh throughout his career.

Dr. Singh's personal values, shaped by his early life in rural Punjab, guided his leadership style. Integrity, hard work, and humility were the core tenets of his character. His emphasis on education, perseverance, and the importance of making decisions for the long-term welfare of the nation were traits he inherited from his family. His deeply ingrained sense of duty and commitment to public service were not simply professional attributes but extended to his personal relationships. This connection between his personal values and his professional life was one of the defining aspects of his leadership.

Throughout his career, Dr. Singh's family remained a source of strength, offering him both the grounding and the resilience necessary to face the political and economic challenges of leading the country. The balance he struck between his public duties and private life reflected the integrity and personal discipline that marked his leadership.

Chapter 14: Leadership Through Silence

Dr. Manmohan Singh's leadership style was often characterised by silence—both in terms of his public communication and his approach to governance. His quiet demean-or, which contrasted sharply with the often loud and dramatic nature of Indian politics, became one of his defining traits. In an environment where political leaders were often judged by their speeches and fiery rhetoric, Singh's silent leadership proved to be both a strength and a source of criticism.

His style was grounded in humility. He rarely sought the limelight, preferring to focus on the work at hand rather than engaging in political theatrics. This made him an ideal technocrat for the post-liberalisation era when India needed pragmatic, result-oriented leadership. Singh's strength lay in his ability to listen, analyse, and then act, often without the fanfare that usually accompanied major political decisions. He focused on substantive governance, rather than cultivating a personal image in the media.

However, Singh's silence was often misunderstood. While his approach worked well in terms of policy implementation, it led to political and media criticism. His quiet nature was sometimes seen as a sign of weakness, and his reluctance to defend his decisions publicly was interpreted as indecisiveness. Critics argued that his reticence left him vulnerable to attacks and allowed others to overshadow his work. In contrast, his supporters viewed his silence as a deliberate strategy to avoid unnecessary political posturing and to allow the work itself to speak for him.

His leadership through silence was not a passive one. On the contrary, it required an immense amount of discipline, self-control, and confidence. Singh did not engage in political mudslinging or seek to score points for personal gain. Instead, he let his policies, including his landmark economic reforms, define his legacy. However, this style also meant that when challenges arose, such as corruption scandals during his second term, his lack of vocal defence left him exposed. His critics often used his silence to question his involvement or responsibility, further complicating the perception of his leadership.

Dr. Singh's leadership model—marked by silence and introspection—was an unconventional approach in Indian politics. His philosophy was that actions should speak louder than words, and that meaningful governance is rooted in pragmatism rather than populism. This quiet approach to leadership was emblematic of his character: disciplined, thoughtful, and focused on the long-term betterment of the nation rather than short-term political gains.

Chapter 15: Vision for India

Dr. Manmohan Singh's vision for India was deeply rooted in his belief in economic growth, social justice, and national self-reliance. His leadership was driven by a strong commitment to modernising India's economy while ensuring that the benefits of growth were equitably distributed across society. This vision, while ambitious, was rooted in his personal experiences and his understanding of India's historical challenges.

At the heart of Dr. Singh's vision was the idea of economic liberalisation, which he saw as the gateway to India's future. He believed that for India to emerge as a global power, it needed to shed its protectionist economic policies, integrate with the global economy, and allow market forces to drive growth. His support for policies that promoted foreign investment, trade liberalisation, and industrial growth were designed to make India an economic powerhouse.

However, Singh's vision went beyond mere economic growth. He was deeply concerned with the social fabric of India and the need to ensure that growth benefited all sections of society. His vision for India was one where poverty was eradicated, social welfare schemes were strengthened, and rural areas experienced the same benefits of development as urban centres. He sought to balance India's growing economy with a commitment to inclusive growth that uplifted the marginalised and provided opportunities for all.

Singh's emphasis on equity was visible in policies like MGNREGA and the RTI, which aimed at empowering the poorest and most vulnerable populations. He envisioned a country where access to basic needs like education, healthcare, and employment were not limited by caste, creed, or geographical location. For Dr. Singh, development was not just about economic indicators, but also about ensuring that every citizen had a fair chance to succeed and prosper.

As India moved further into the 21st century, Dr. Singh was committed to expanding the country's role in global affairs. His vision was one of a confident, self-reliant India that was integrated into the world economy, and he saw India's global standing as directly linked to its economic and technological advancements. During his tenure, India saw rapid growth in the information technology sector, advancements in nuclear energy, and a burgeoning middle class—all part of his broader vision for a modern, progressive nation.

Yet, Singh's vision was not without its challenges. Balancing growth with equity proved to be a difficult task, as India's rapid economic rise also led to greater income disparity and regional inequalities. While policies like MGNREGA were aimed at reducing these disparities, the challenges of corruption, inefficient implementation, and political opposition often undermined their full potential.

Dr. Singh's leadership was characterised by a vision of a strong and self-sufficient India—one that could compete on the global stage while lifting its citizens out of poverty. His commitment to inclusive growth, social welfare, and long-term sustainability continues to shape discussions on India's future development. His tenure may have been marked by economic challenges, but his vision for India remains an enduring part of his legacy, inspiring future generations to build a prosperous and equitable nation.

———●———

"WHILE WE HAVE MADE significant progress, the fight against poverty and inequality remains a challenge. We must continue to focus on inclusive growth to ensure that the benefits of development reach everyone."

-Dr Manmohan Singh

Part V: Legacy and Reflections
Chapter 16: The Legacy of Liberalisation

Dr. Manmohan Singh's reforms in the early 1990s marked the beginning of a new era for India—one that embraced economic liberalisation and global integration. These reforms, initiated during his tenure as Finance Minister in 1991, laid the foundation for modern India's rapid economic growth. His policies reshaped the Indian economy, making it more competitive, efficient, and integrated with the global marketplace.

At the heart of Dr. Singh's legacy lies the dismantling of India's protectionist trade policies, the opening up of markets, and the encouragement of foreign investment. By reducing tariffs, cutting government controls, and devaluing the rupee, Singh sought to break free from the constraints of the past. His reforms opened doors for private sector growth, led to a surge in foreign direct investment, and paved the way for India to become one of the world's fastest-growing economies. These changes transformed sectors such as technology, manufacturing, and services, positioning India as a global player in the 21st century.

Perspectives on Dr. Singh's legacy from economists, politicians, and historians offer a broad spectrum of views. Many economists credit Singh with saving India from economic stagnation, highlighting his role as the architect of the liberalisation policies that allowed the country to transition from a state-controlled economy to a more market-driven one. His focus on fiscal discipline, inflation control, and macroeconomic stability set the stage for India's economic boom in the following decades.

Politicians, however, offer a more nuanced perspective. While many acknowledge Singh's economic vision, his political career often faced challenges. As Prime Minister, his leadership was sometimes overshadowed by coalition politics and controversies surrounding corruption scandals. Nevertheless, his commitment to economic reforms remained a cornerstone of his legacy, with many viewing him as the quiet, behind-the-scenes architect of India's rise.

Historians, too, recognise Dr. Singh's pivotal role in transforming India. They highlight how his reforms helped the country break free from the stagnation of the post-independence era, enabling the next generation of leaders to steer India toward global prominence. Today, India stands as the world's fifth-largest economy, and much of that growth can be attributed to the groundwork laid by Singh during the 1990s.

The legacy of liberalisation, then, is not just one of economic transformation—it is the story of how Dr. Singh reshaped India's place in the world and laid the foundation for the India we know today.

Chapter 17: Public Perception and Criticism

Dr. Manmohan Singh's tenure as Prime Minister of India was met with both admiration and criticism. While his economic reforms garnered widespread praise, his political leadership often faced challenges, and public perception of his effectiveness as a leader remained mixed throughout his time in office.

On one hand, Singh's quiet demeanour and technocratic background earned him respect among many economists and intellectuals, who admired his expertise and vision. His emphasis on policy over personality was seen as a refreshing change from the often noisy, populist style of politics. As Prime Minister, Singh focused on long-term strategies for economic growth, social welfare, and modernisation. His commitment to social programs like the Right to Information Act (RTI) and the Mahatma Gandhi National Rural Employment Guarantee Act (MGNREGA) made him a leader who sought to balance economic progress with social justice.

However, Singh also faced criticism for his perceived lack of political engagement and inability to project himself as a strong, decisive leader. His tenure as Prime Minister was often seen as overshadowed by the influence of Sonia Gandhi, the Congress Party leader, and he was criticised for not being more assertive in matters of governance. His relationship with the Gandhi family, while cordial, was often portrayed in the media as one of dependence, leading to questions about his authority and political independence.

Additionally, Singh's handling of the UPA-II government's second term was marred by corruption scandals, which damaged his public image. Although Singh himself was never directly implicated in the scandals, his inability to address them effectively led to questions about his leadership and accountability. His critics argued that his silence on matters of corruption, combined with his passive style, made it difficult for his administration to regain public trust.

In light of recent developments, there has been a reevaluation of Dr. Singh's legacy. Many now view his leadership in a more favourable light, especially when compared to more recent political trends. The current political landscape, characterised by a more polarised and assertive style of governance, has led to a reassessment of Singh's approach. In an era where populist rhetoric often overshadows substantive policy, Singh's quiet, policy-driven leadership stands out as an example of integrity and commitment to the nation's long-term growth.

Chapter 18: The Global Statesman

While Dr. Manmohan Singh's domestic policies were crucial in shaping modern India, his contributions on the global stage were equally significant. As Prime Minister, Singh played a key role in reshaping India's foreign policy and strengthening its international relations, particularly with the United States, China, and India's neighbours.

One of Singh's most notable achievements in foreign policy was his role in the Indo-US nuclear deal. His decision to pursue a civilian nuclear agreement with the United States marked a significant departure from India's traditional policy of nuclear self-sufficiency and was a bold move that opened up new avenues for India's energy security and international cooperation. The deal, which was finalised in 2008, allowed India to gain access to nuclear technology and fuel, which had previously been denied due to sanctions. This not only boosted India's energy capabilities but also solidified its position as a rising global power.

Singh also worked to strengthen India's relations with China, navigating the complexities of both cooperation and competition. Despite historical tensions, Singh sought to engage with China through dialogue and diplomacy, understanding the importance of economic and strategic relations with the world's second-largest economy. During his tenure, trade between India and China grew significantly, and the two countries entered into agreements to manage border disputes and deepen economic ties.

On India's immediate borders, Singh emphasised strengthening relationships with neighbouring countries, particularly Pakistan, Sri Lanka, and Nepal. While India-Pakistan relations remained contentious during his tenure, Singh consistently advocated for dialogue and peaceful coexistence. His approach to diplomacy was characterised by pragmatism, emphasising India's growing stature as a regional leader committed to stability and cooperation in South Asia.

Dr. Singh's foreign policy approach was defined by realism and strategic foresight. He recognised the shifting dynamics of global power and worked to position India as an influential player in international affairs. His efforts in strengthening India's ties with key global players, including the United States, China, and neighbouring countries, helped shape India's rise as a prominent voice in global governance.

Chapter 19: A Life of Integrity

Dr. Manmohan Singh's life and career were defined by a steadfast commitment to integrity, humility, and dedication to public service. In an era where politics is often associated with power struggles, corruption, and populism, Singh's career stands as a testament to the values of honesty and ethical leadership.

From his early days as an economist to his tenure as Prime Minister, Singh adhered to principles that emphasised the greater good over personal gain. His honesty in government was unquestioned, and his reputation for integrity earned him respect both domestically and internationally. His refusal to indulge in political manoeuvring, his focus on policy over personal ambition, and his commitment to serving the nation rather than seeking personal power made him a rare figure in the world of Indian politics.

Throughout his career, Dr. Singh remained steadfast in his belief that leaders should serve the public with dedication and accountability. Unlike many of his contemporaries, he never sought to cultivate a larger-than-life persona or use his position for personal enrichment. His leadership was based on the idea that true power lies in service to others, not in the pursuit of self-interest. This sense of integrity was reflected in his actions, from his handling of the economic crisis of 1991 to his management of government scandals during his time as Prime Minister.

Dr. Singh's life of integrity offers valuable lessons for leaders today. In a world where political rhetoric and personal gain often overshadow the needs of the people, his example serves as a reminder of the power of ethical leadership. His commitment to transparency, honesty, and service to the nation provides a blueprint for leaders who wish to lead with integrity, focusing on the welfare of the public rather than personal ambitions.

"A THRIVING DEMOCRACY in India is central to the success of the economic reforms we have undertaken. It is the strength of our democracy that allows for continued progress."
    -Dr Manmohan Singh

Conclusion

Chapter 20: India's Silent Revolution

Dr. Manmohan Singh's journey from a quiet scholar to a transformative leader is nothing short of remarkable. His tenure as Finance Minister and Prime Minister marked a period of profound change for India, both economically and politically. As we reflect on his life and legacy, it is clear that his impact on India's development is indelible, shaping the country's trajectory for generations to come.

India's economic transformation in the 1990s is perhaps the most visible aspect of Dr. Singh's legacy. His reforms, though initially met with resistance, became the cornerstone of modern India's economic success. By introducing liberalisation, deregulation, and globalisation into India's economy, Singh helped the country break free from the constraints of its past and set it on a path of rapid growth. His policies fostered an environment that encouraged entrepreneurship, attracted foreign investment, and positioned India as a global economic power. Today, India is one of the world's largest and fastest-growing economies, and much of that success can be traced back to the groundwork laid by Singh in the 1990s.

Yet, Dr. Singh's impact extends beyond the economic realm. He was also a crucial figure in strengthening India's democratic institutions. Despite navigating through complex coalition politics, Singh remained committed to the principles of governance that prioritised transparency, integrity, and social welfare. His introduction of landmark initiatives such as the Right to Information Act (RTI) and the Mahatma Gandhi National Rural Employment Guarantee Act (MGNREGA) laid the foundation for a more inclusive India, where the government was held accountable to its citizens. His leadership style, characterised by humility, thoughtfulness, and patience, demonstrated that governance is not about projecting power but about creating a vision for the country and working tirelessly to achieve it.

However, Singh's journey was not without its challenges. His leadership was often overshadowed by controversies, particularly during his second term as Prime Minister, when corruption scandals tarnished the UPA government's image. Yet, Singh's response to these challenges—marked by a refusal to succumb to populism or political opportunism—reflected his steadfast commitment to the principles of integrity and service. While some critics questioned his effectiveness as a political leader, his economic reforms and diplomatic achievements cemented his place in history as one of India's most consequential figures.

In the final analysis, the lessons from Dr. Singh's journey are profound. His life teaches us that true leadership is not about grandstanding or seeking recognition, but about quietly and persistently pursuing what is best for the nation. His ability to navigate political complexities, his unwavering commitment to reform, and his focus on economic and social equity provide a blueprint for future leaders. Singh's legacy reminds us that leadership can—and should—be rooted in humility, vision, and an unshakable dedication to public service.

As we move into the future, the story of Dr. Manmohan Singh and his silent revolution remains an inspiration for those who believe in the power of transformative leadership. His contributions to India's economic growth, democratic stability, and global stature continue to shape the nation's development, leaving an enduring legacy that will be felt for many decades to come. Dr. Singh's journey is a reminder that even in a world of noisy politics and turbulent change, quiet leaders who put the nation's interests first can make the most lasting and profound impact.

India's silent revolution, led by a man of quiet determination and intellect, continues to resonate in the corridors of power and among the millions of people whose lives were transformed by the reforms he championed. His story is not just the history of a nation's economic rise, but the legacy of a leader who believed that change can happen without fanfare, and that true power lies in the quiet pursuit of the greater good.

"Economic growth is not a luxury; it is a necessity. It is the only way we can overcome poverty, create jobs, and ensure a better life for our people."

DR MANMOHAN SINGH